Wheels Keep Turning

Mick Manning • Brita Granström

W
FRANKLIN WATTS
LONDON•SYDNEY

Long ago an idea began
turning in human heads…
Like the moon's full face…

Like a sycamore seed
spinning in the
wind…

2

Like a log rolling underfoot…

That idea was a wheel – and
once it started it couldn't be stopped.

Wheels keep turning!
Logs made into
rollers pulling heavy
stones...

People first used logs
as rollers to move huge
blocks of stone over
7000 years ago.

In Britain 3000 years later,

people moved stones in this way to build Stonehenge.

Wheels keep turning! Spinning wet clay to make pots and bowls. Then cartwheels bumping and jolting the pots to market…

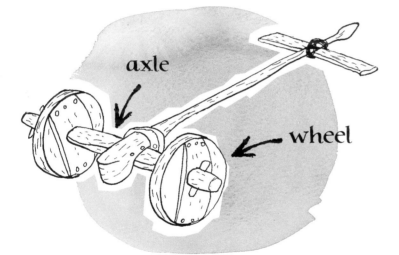

axle

wheel

About 5500 years ago, in the Middle East, someone took slices off the rollers and put them on a rod to spin round. These were wheels on an axle.

First came the potter's wheel . . .

Then cartwheels. Perhaps cartwheels were based on the potter's wheel?

Wheels keep turning!
Wheelbarrows trundling along,
shifting heavy loads of mud... or stone...

Ropes running round pulleys
to lift heavy loads...

The Chinese invented wheelbarrows about 2000 years ago.

8

Pulleys are also useful on building sites. They help lift up heavy loads.

9

Wheels keep turning!
Making chariots thunder
behind galloping horses!

About 4000 years ago,
Egyptian chariots had wheels
with spokes, which made the
chariots lighter and faster.

Later in Europe,

the Celts became experts in making strong wheels - and fast chariots.

The Romans invented an upright water-wheel 2000 years ago.

By medieval times, there were watermills all over Europe.

12

Wheels keep turning!
Water-wheel paddles
spinning faster and faster.
Windmill sails twisting round
and round.

Driving cog wheels –
wheels with teeth! They
drive the grindstones, to
make flour for our bread.

Europeans first used wind power about 800 years ago. The wind blew round the sails of a windmill, which turned the cog wheels and grindstones inside.

13

Wheels keep turning.
On the town hall,
or in our pocket.

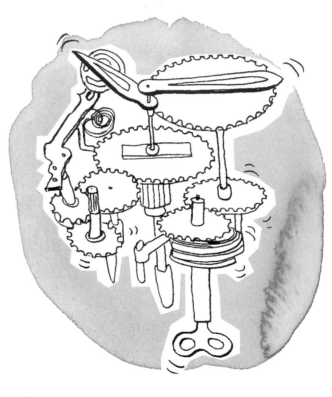

The cog wheels in a clock turn at different speeds. A wound-up spring sets them going. Mechanical clocks first appeared about 700 years ago.

Ticking and turning,
as regular as clockwork!

Clockwork can make many
things work, from clocks
to wind up toys; there are
even clockwork radios.

15

Wheels keep turning,
and turning and turning!

Stagecoaches with wheels
wrapped in iron that
bump and rattle,
day and night, taking
passengers and post
across the country.

The iron 'tyres' on the coach
wheel protected it from
damage – but it was
a very bumpy ride.

Highwaymen made a living from coaches - they robbed the passengers!

Wheels keep turning!
Out in the fields clever new
machines are trundling;
they sow…
and mow…
and thresh…

About 300 years ago, wheels helped bring about great changes in farming ~ the 'Agricultural Revolution' began!

18

Farming machines were invented to make things easier and quicker for farmers. Fewer people were needed to work in the fields.

a threshing machine

Wheels keep turning. Inside dark, dirty mills, cogs and pulleys turning oily machines, spinning cotton and wool. Wheels within wheels within wheels, thundering and clattering all day long!

spinning jenny

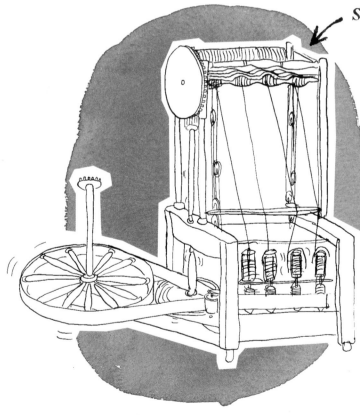

In the Industrial Revolution, factories full of machines, powered by water and steam, spun and wove ~ and made more parts for more machines to make more things. Mass production took off!

20

The **word** *revolution* itself comes from the word revolve!

This is the Mallard. Built in 1938, it was the fastest steam train ever.

Wheels keep turning!
Iron wheels along an iron track.
Steam trains chuffing and puffing…

The steam train was invented in 1804 in Britain. Trains travelling on a special metal track were ideal for transporting cloth, coal and other goods.

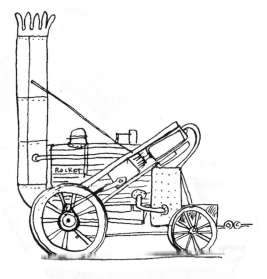

In 1829 Stephenson's Rocket won a competition as the best locomotive engine to pull the carriages along.

Wheels keep turning. Combustion engines coughing and spluttering, with pistons pushing crankshafts, turning wheels… Driving the first motor-cars along bumpy roads – honk, honk!

The first motor-car was built in Germany in 1885.

Rubber tyres filled with air gave a softer ride.

Wheels keep turning!
Fairground wheels
and roundabouts –
funfair rides for
everyone!

The London Eye was a huge Ferris wheel built to celebrate the year 2000 in Britain.

Funfairs became very popular in the first half of the 20th century.

Wheels keep turning . . .

Rollers rotating

Chariots charging →

Water wheels whirling

Clocks ticking →

Potter's wheels revolving

Wheelbarrows rolling

Coaches bumping

Carts trundling →

Machines ploughing →

Cars honking →

Big wheels twirling →

Steam trains puffing →

Factories spinning ↑

Wheels still turning!

29

Helpful words

Agricultural Revolution The great changes in farming that began in Britain about 300 years ago. Fewer people were needed to farm the land. See pages 18, 19.

Axle The rod or pole around which a wheel turns. See page 6.

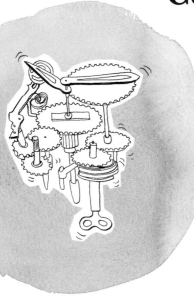

Cog wheel A wheel with a series of teeth around its edge. Cog wheels are often called gear wheels. See pages 12, 13, 14, 15.

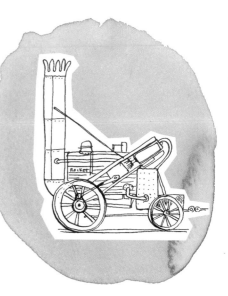

Engine A machine (or part of a machine) that makes things work and move.

A combustion engine runs by burning fuel such as petrol inside it. See pages 23, 24.

Grindstones Heavy stones that grind corn into flour. See pages 12, 13.

Industrial Revolution The great changes that took place to people's lives in Britain (and later elsewhere) from about 1760. It was caused by the new ways of making things, particularly cotton and wool yarn, quickly and cheaply in factories. See pages 20, 21.

Mill A place where corn is ground or things are made (like a factory). See pages 12, 13, 20, 21.

Mow To cut grass, hay or crops. See pages 18, 19.

Pulley A simple machine which uses a rope running round a wheel to move or lift something. The pulley wheel usually has a groove around its edge to keep the rope in position. See pages 8, 9.

Sow To plant seeds. See page 18.

Steam The hot gas or vapour made by boiling water. It is used to power machines and engines. See page 20.

Thresh To separate the corn or seed from the rest of the wheat plant. See pages 18, 19.

For Rachel, Philippa, Jonathan, Robert,
Mariesa and all the Watts 'Wonderwise' team

This edition 2005

First published by Franklin Watts
338 Euston Road, London, NW1 3BH

Franklin Watts Australia
Level 17/207 Kent Street, Sydney, NSW 2000

Text and illustrations © 2000 Mick Manning and Brita Granström
Notes and activities © 2005 Franklin Watts
Series editor: Rachel Cooke
Art director: Jonathan Hair
Consultant: Andrew Nahum

The illustrations in this book were made by Brita and Mick
Find out more about Mick and Brita on www.mickandbrita.com

Printed in Singapore
A CIP catalogue record is available from the British Library.
Dewey Classification 621
ISBN 978 0 7496 6223 3

Franklin Watts is a division of Hachette Children's Books, an Hachette
Livre UK company.

Go through the book again
and look for this mouse.

How many times can you spot him?